TREASURY OF LITERATURE

WRITER'S JOURNAL

OUT OF THIS WORLD

Acknowledgments appear on page 106.
Printed in the United States of America

ISBN 0-15-301275-7
7 8 9 10 11 12   030   03 02 01 00 99 98

HARCOURT BRACE & COMPANY

Orlando   Atlanta   Austin   Boston   San Francisco   Chicago   Dallas   New York
Toronto   London

CONTENTS

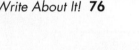

UNIT ONE

CHALLENGES

Read about these "Challenges."
Then turn to page 6.

★ **Roberto Clemente** ★

AMAZING ATHLETE

When she was 5 years old, Sarah Billmeier learned she had bone cancer. To save her life, doctors had to amputate her left leg and remove her left hip.

Sarah didn't let that stop her from playing sports—lots of them. Today, she is a sports-minded freshman at Yarmouth High School in Yarmouth, Maine. She competes for an age-group swim team, plays second base and outfield for her school softball team, and is a goalie for her school soccer team. She plays all of these sports on one leg. She doesn't even use crutches or an artificial leg.

from "Busting Loose!" by John Grossmann in
SPORTS ILLUSTRATED FOR KIDS, September 1991

Becoming an American

I stood on the deck of the ship, shivering as dawn crested the skyline of New York City. It was June 3, 1959, and after ten days crossing the Atlantic we were in America. My grandmother wrapped a sweater around me and my seven-year-old brother, Alexandre.

The city seemed too large and too beautiful to be the work of man. I had lived all my 11 years as a Russian refugee in Morocco, knowing I could never be Moroccan. Now I felt a pang of fear. Could I ever be American?

from "How I Became an American"
by Constantin Galskoy in *Reader's Digest*, August 1991

Ordinary Jack

Ordinary Jack, that's me. It's what they should've christened me—Ordinary Jack Matthew Bagthorpe, with an e.

There were four Bagthorpe children, and the other three were always winning prizes and medals, and William, the eldest, had got to the point where he was winning cups, silver ones, for the sideboard, and little shields with his name engraved on them.

You're immortal if your name gets put on cups and shields, thought Jack moodily. I'll never be immortal.

—from ORDINARY JACK
by Helen Cresswell

WRITE ABOUT CHALLENGES

Do one of these:

Pretend you are making a film to show outsiders what your school is like. What will you show in your film? List the scenes you would include.

Imagine that you are approaching your school for the first time. Write a paragraph describing what you see and hear.

by_____
(your name)

Welcome Club

In "The Kid in the Red Jacket," Howard learned to adjust to being a new kid in school. Now he and some of his friends have formed a club to help other new kids. Imagine that you are a member of the club. What will you do to make new students feel welcome at your school?

ORGANIZATION: Welcome Club

TO: All Members

SUBJECT: Actions we will take to help kids feel at home here

MEMBER: _____

(your name)

WHAT-A-DAY!

Can you remember a day when it seemed that everything went wrong? Write a paragraph telling what happened that day. You may write about a real experience or one you have imagined. Be sure to use causes and effects to show why things happen in your story.

_____
_____
_____
_____
_____
_____
_____
_____
_____
_____
_____
_____
_____
_____

written by_____

(your name)

WHAT A PLACE!

Baseball . . . the Dodgers . . . Jackie Robinson! In "In the Year of the Boar and Jackie Robinson," many things in America seem strange to Shirley. Imagine that you are Shirley and you are writing a letter to a friend in China who has never been to the United States. What will you tell him or her about your experiences in America? Write your letter in the space below.

(your name)

PLEASE REPORT TO THE OFFICE

That's you!

Your name has just been called over the loudspeaker, followed by the words **"PLEASE REPORT TO THE OFFICE IMMEDIATELY."** Write the first few paragraphs of a journal entry that begins with your being called to the office. Be sure to include information about what you say and do that will help readers draw conclusions about your feelings and predict what might happen next.

Journal of

_____

(your name)

Date:

Ask Pedro

Pedro wants to be recognized as an individual. Instead of the questions in the poem, what would you ask Pedro in order to find out who he is and what he is really like? List your questions below.

1. _____

_____

_____

2. _____

_____

3. _____

_____

_____

_____

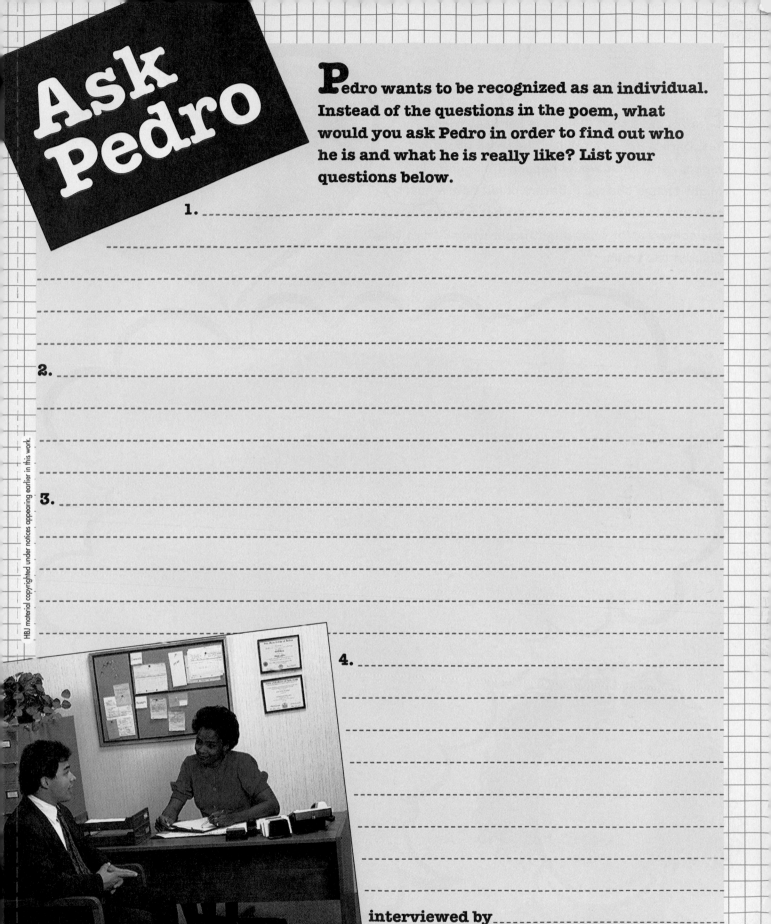

4. _____

_____

_____

_____

_____

_____

interviewed by _____
(your name)

Barbra says that Claudia is her best friend. Yet, Barbra doesn't tell her the truth about her report card. What would happen if she did? How might things change if Barbra could have a heart-to-heart talk with Claudia about her feelings? Write the conversation that might occur when Barbra tells Claudia the truth.

A Heart-to-Heart Chat

In "Pride of Puerto Rico," several people developed opinions about young Roberto Clemente. Have these people tell what they think about Roberto, and why. Draw yourself saying what you think, too.

Have Your SAY

Don Melchor

Señora Cáceres

Señor Marín

_____
(your name)

Choose a Day

Think about the characters in "Sarah, Plain and Tall"—Sarah, Papa, Anna, and Caleb. Write a journal entry for one of the characters, describing a day soon after Sarah's arrival. Include what your character might say about one or more of the other characters.

_____

_____

_____

_____

_____

_____

_____

_____

_____

_____

_____

_____

_____

_____

_____

_____

(your name)

SARAH, PLAIN & TALL THE TV SERIES

Become a casting director for "Sarah, Plain and Tall: The TV Series." Who would you cast in the lead roles of Sarah, Papa, Anna, and Caleb? Think about the actor's age, physical appearance, voice quality, and personality. Write a memo to the series director naming your choices and the reasons for making them.

Sarah:_____
_____
_____

Papa:_____
_____
_____

Anna:_____
_____
_____

Caleb:_____
_____
_____
_____

Signed_____, Casting Director
(your name)

Imagine That!

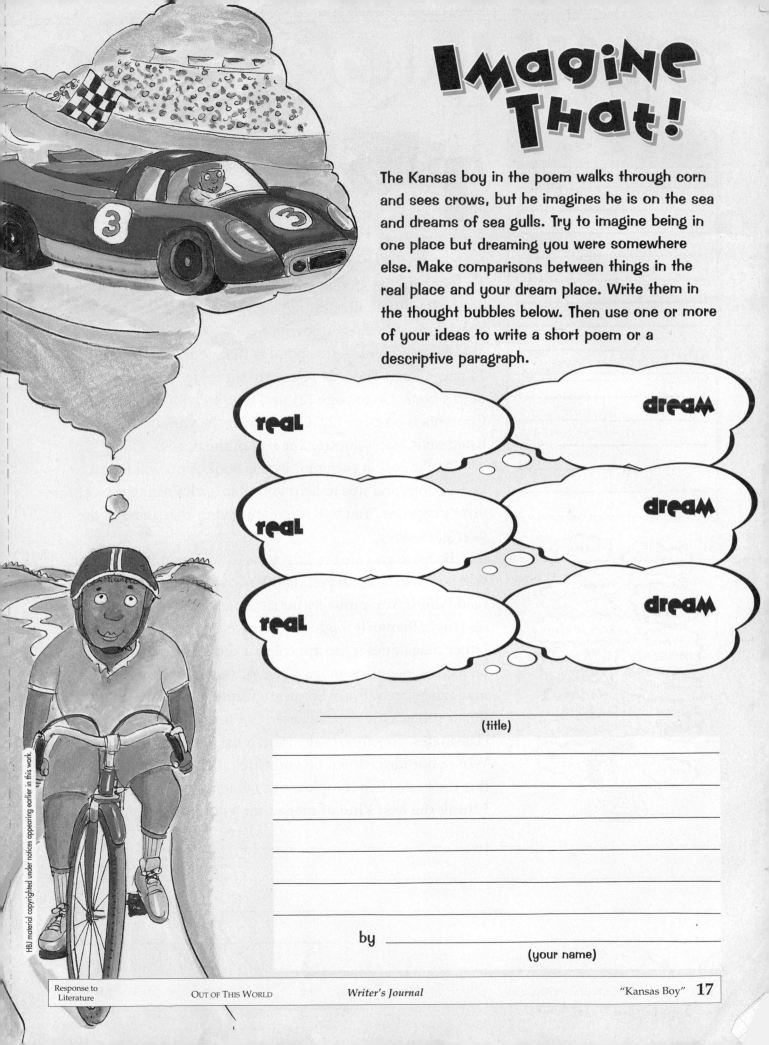

The Kansas boy in the poem walks through corn and sees crows, but he imagines he is on the sea and dreams of sea gulls. Try to imagine being in one place but dreaming you were somewhere else. Make comparisons between things in the real place and your dream place. Write them in the thought bubbles below. Then use one or more of your ideas to write a short poem or a descriptive paragraph.

real

dream

real

dream

real

dream

_____
(title)

_____

_____

_____

_____

_____

by _____
(your name)

MAKING YOUR

IDEA PAD

_____

_____

_____

_____

_____

_____

_____

_____

_____

_____

_____

_____

SKIING · CARS · GARDENING · FAMILY LIFE · SCHOOL EVENTS · STAMP COLLECTING · AROUND TOWN · COMPUTERS · TROPICAL FISH · OUTER SPACE · PHOTOGRAPHY · MUSIC · MOVIES

Today is your first day on the job as Editor-in-Chief of your own magazine. No one works for you yet, so you have to do everything—page design, writing, and illustrations. Think about the kind of magazine you'd like to have. Imagine yourself writing, illustrating, and putting together this very special magazine—your own.

All you know at this point is that your magazine will be 24 pages long. These 24 pages are set aside for you at the end of this book. Go to page 121 and take a look. The Table of Contents is on page 122. Glance over the variety of articles listed on it. Look through the rest of the pages.

At the end of each unit in this book , you will find instructions and tips to help you plan each writing project for your magazine. You will be creating your magazine as the year goes along.

Because you are the Editor-in-Chief, what the magazine will be about is up to you. Think about magazines you have read before. You probably noticed that some magazines have one main theme. It might be travel, nature, science, or fashion. Other magazines try to appeal to a certain audience, such as teenagers, people your own age, or senior citizens. Some magazines are serious. Some are funny. Some have many illustrations. Others have none. Get together with a few classmates. Together, brainstorm a list of magazine ideas. Write your ideas down on your Idea Pad. Choose the one you like the best. Then complete this sentence:

I think the best kind of magazine would be one that _____

_____

_____

_____

_____ .

OWN MAGAZINE

Naming Your Magazine

What will you call your magazine? Remember that your title should give a clue about the theme of the magazine. Think about some magazine titles that you know. What do they have in common? Do they have many words, a few words, or just one word? Do they have any punctuation? List some possible titles for your magazine. Then choose your favorite and write it here:

_____

Now that you have chosen your title, think about the cover design. What colors, if any, will you use? What kind of art, if any, will you use? What kind of lettering will you use? Will you list any part of your Table of Contents on the cover? Sketch out some designs on a separate piece of paper to see what works.

MEETING THE EDITOR-IN-CHIEF

People who read magazines usually want to know something about the Editor-in-Chief. One magazine page is set aside for you to introduce yourself. What will you say? Will you talk about your early childhood, or will you focus on your goals for the future? Will you include a picture? Before you write a draft of your introduction, think about these questions:

- **How would you describe yourself?**

- **What do you think about the idea of this magazine?**

- **Why do you want to create a magazine on this topic or for this audience?**

- **What has happened in your life that makes you interested in this topic?**

- **What other details might your readers be interested in?**

Think about what artwork, colors, and lettering on a cover would best attract a reader's attention.

Go to page 121 to publish your cover.

Make your introduction really express your thoughts. Let your reader get to know you. Tell the reader something about yourself.

Ready? Go to page 123 to publish your introduction.

MAKING YOUR

1 Writing an In-Depth News Article: Choosing a Topic

The first article in your magazine will be an in-depth news article. There are four pages in your magazine set aside for this article. Turn to pages 124–127 to have a look.

Your first step is to choose a topic. The main thing is for you to be enthusiastic about the topic. That way, you will be able to write an interesting, exciting article. Think for a moment about the theme of your magazine. Ask yourself these questions:

- **What kind of news is there about this theme?**

- **What details about my theme am I most interested in?**

- **What is happening that is new in this area?**

Brainstorm a list of ideas. Ask classmates for suggestions. Draw a web, like the one shown. Look over the ideas in your web. Which ideas really interest you? Which ones are interesting enough for an in-depth news article?

Choosing a good topic is the most important step. Take your time. Then write your idea for your article on the lines below:

_____

_____

_____

_____

_____

_____

OWN MAGAZINE

2 GATHERING FACTS FOR YOUR ARTICLE

Do some research for your article to add to your knowledge. Use the following sources:

- Library, for background: books, magazines, and encyclopedias
- People with knowledge about your topic
- The media, for current information: radio, TV, and newspapers

Take notes on index cards while doing research! Gather more information than you can possibly use for your article.

IS YOUR TOPIC TOO BIG TO COVER?

NARROW IT DOWN.

3 Writing and Revising a Draft/ Choosing Illustrations

The next step is to organize your notes. Put related index cards into separate piles. Using facts from your notes, write a first draft. Let your ideas flow easily. Don't worry about details of style and grammar right now. You can go back later to rethink and revise.

When you finish your draft, read it to a classmate. Together, talk about how you can make your article even better.

If you'd like to include illustrations, you can draw them, cut them out from magazines, or make photocopies from books.

Your readers will want to know more about the illustrations. Don't forget to add a caption to each one. Does your article quote any other source? Don't forget to give credit for other people's words.

Ready for the next steps? Go to page 124.

Don't forget the five Ws of a news story: *who, what, where, when,* and *why.*

HBJ material copyrighted under notices appearing earlier in this work.

UNIT TWO

TRIALS

Read all about "Trials."
Then turn to page 24.

Riddle

Riddle my this, riddle my that — guess my riddle or perhaps not. Boy is sent for something; something comes back before boy — why?

from WHEN I DANCE: POEMS by JAMES BERRY

— Boy climbs tree, picks coconut and drops it.

The Ongloti Language

Can you read Ongloti? You can if you are reading this!

English is full of different letter combinations with the same sounds. The *o* in *women* sounds like the *i* in *win*. And the *ti* in *station* sounds like the *sh* in *shadow*. So, if you spell *English* with the *o* from *women* for the two *i* sounds and the *ti* from *station* for the *sh* sound, you get *Ongloti*!

Here are some other letter combinations and their sounds: the *ei* in *neighbor* sounds like the *a* in *nay*; the *o* in *one* sounds like the *w* in *won*; the *gh* in *tough* sounds like the *f* in *muff*; and the *or* in *work* sounds like the *ir* in *sir*. Keeping these in mind, can you figure out the following Ongloti words? There is a hint with each one.

1	oond	It can move things.
2	tielgh	You put things on it.
3	gheid	This often happens to clothes.
4	ghorst	It's number one.

From *The Puzzle Book: The 1982 Childcraft Annual.* ©1982 by World Book, Inc. Reprinted by permission of World Book Publishing.

Answers: 1 wind; 2 shelf; 3 fade; 4 first

Lost: Amelia Earhart

Commander Thompson was tense.

At 2:45 A.M., the voice of the famous American pilot had piped through the crackling static on wavelength 3105 into the radio room of the U.S. Coast Guard cutter *Itasca*. "Cloudy and overcast," she said, "...headwinds."

Frustration and anxiety in the cutter's radio room mounted. What was wrong? Why wouldn't Amelia Earhart give them her position? Didn't she know? Worse yet, couldn't she hear them? They had to know where she was!

The whole world was watching this flight.... The radio link was vital—and it didn't seem to be working!

from *Lost...and Never Found* by Anita Gustafson

WRITE ABOUT TRIALS

Do one of these:

Imagine that you will face a small problem on your way home from school. Write about this problem and what you will do to solve it.

Use Ongloti words to write puzzles for a friend to solve. Be sure to keep your own list of words as a key to the letter combinations and sounds.

by _____

(your name)

STORM

How I Heard About the Storm

I, _____,
(your name)

_____
_____
_____
_____
_____
_____

How the Clouds Looked

_____
_____
_____
_____
_____
_____
_____
_____

What I Did During the Storm

_____
_____
_____
_____
_____
_____

How I Felt During the Storm

_____
_____
_____
_____
_____
_____
_____

Think about a storm that you have read about or seen. Under each heading, write sentences, using vivid, descriptive words. Help someone else understand what the storm was like and how you felt about it.

Storm Coming!

The kinds of weather you read about in "Storms" can be frightening. Imagine that a thunderstorm or tornado struck near you. How did you feel? What did you do? Write a beginning paragraph for a journal entry about your experience. Be sure to use vivid descriptive words.

date_____

_____

_____

_____

_____

_____

_____

_____

_____

_____

_____

_____

_____

_____

_____

_____

_____

's Journal

(your name)

You're the expert! Write a short magazine article about your town, school, or classroom. Include your own opinions as well as facts to express your views on the subject you have chosen.

An Expert's Views

------------------------------ (title) ------------------------------

----

----

by ------------- (your name)

The Day After

If you were a television news reporter interviewing Dan the day after the tornado, what questions would you ask him? Write your questions on the lines that begin with the word REPORTER. On the lines that begin with DAN, write the answers you think Dan would give.

REPORTER: _____

_____

DAN: _____

_____

REPORTER: _____

_____

DAN: _____

_____

REPORTER: _____

_____

DAN: _____

_____

REPORTER: _____

_____

DAN: _____

_____

REPORTER (ending interview): This has been _____

(your name)

_____

WHAT NEXT?

Read the story beginning below. Think about what might happen next. Then write two more paragraphs for the story, telling about the next two things that happen. Remember to place your story events in order and use sequence words and phrases.

SOME CATCH!

The sun slanted lower and lower and lower through the trees, making the lake sparkle deep blue. Jana sighed. It was getting late and time to head back to camp. "Just once more," she said to herself.

One last time Jana baited her hook and dropped her fishing line into the water. As usual . . . nothing. Then, just as she was starting to reel in the line, she felt a tug. Jana leaped up in excitement. The pole was almost jerked from her hand!

Written by

STRUCK!

"**T**ornado! Poems" tells how destructive a tornado can be. Imagine that your town has been hit by a tornado. What would your neighborhood be like after the storm? Write your description below.

AFTER THE STORM

by _____
(your name)

Imagine you're going to spend the night in a place that fascinates you. Transport yourself in your imagination to a museum, an amusement park, a department store, or other place of your choice. On the pages below, fill in your plans for spending the night there.

OVERNIGHT VISIT

Where we'll sleep _____

_____

_____

_____

Who will go with me _____

_____

_____

_____

What I'll take _____

_____

_____

_____

What might happen _____

_____

_____

_____

_____

_____

_____

_____

_____

_____

_____

_____

_____

Planned by

_____
(your name)

★ THE ★ DAILY ★ GAZETTE

----

written by _____
(your name)

---   ---

---   ---

---   ---

---   ---

---   ---

---   ---

---   ---

---   ---

---   ---

---   ---

                                                               ----

                                                               ----

                                                               ----

                                                               ----

                                                               ----

Imagine that Claudia and Jamie are found in the museum. Write a newspaper story reporting how they had slipped into the museum and what they did there. Be sure your story answers the questions Who, What, Where, When, How, and Why. Give your story a headline that will catch the reader's attention.

JURY DUTY

In "You Be the Jury," you were a member of the jury. Imagine a telephone conversation between you and a friend after the cases have been settled. How would you answer your friend's questions?

FRIEND: Hey! I heard you were on a jury for that case about the jewelry store robbery! What's it like to be on a jury?

YOU: _____
_____
_____
_____
_____

FRIEND: How did you ever decide whether the defendant was innocent or guilty?

YOU: _____
_____
_____
_____

FRIEND: Being on a jury is an important job. How did you feel about having all that responsibility?

YOU: _____
_____
_____
_____
Member of the Jury: _____
(your name)

FLIGHT!
The Board Game

Conceived and
Designed by _____
                              (your name)

Design a board game called *Flight!* Begin by deciding on the purpose of the game, such as "making the first nonstop flight over the Atlantic Ocean" or "traveling through time from early flying machines to spaceships." Will there be special cards called "Chance" or "Disaster"? The ideas below will help you organize your game plans.

START

| Draw one Up, Up and Away! card | Draw one Oops! card | | | Draw one Up, Up and Away! card | Draw one Oops! card |

The purpose (goal) of the game is

_____

_____

Some spaces on the board will be marked

_____

_____

Draw one Oops! card

Draw one Up, Up and Away! card

Some unusual things about the game will be

_____

_____

Draw one Up, Up and Away! card

Draw one Oops! card

Players will move their game tokens after

_____

_____

The winner is one who _____

_____

_____

| Draw one Oops! card | Draw one Up, Up and Away! card | | | Draw one Oops! card | Draw one Up, Up and Away! card |

BRIAN'S RESCUE

AT THE END

of the selection, Brian is stranded alone in the wilderness. How will searchers find him and rescue him? Brainstorm possible ways that Brian might be rescued.

_____

_____

_____

_____

_____

_____

_____

_____

_____

_____

_____

_____

_____

_____

_____

_____

_____

_____

_____

_____

_____

WRITE A SCENE

Choose one of your ideas on page 35 and create a play scene. Describe the setting briefly. Decide who your cast of characters will be. Make the searchers into intriguing characters and provide a variety of personality types. (Perhaps one is quirky, another funny, and another the strong, silent type.) Interesting characters add pizzazz to a play.

by _____
(your name)

Setting: _____
_____

Cast of Characters: _____

_____

_____

_____

_____

_____

_____

_____

_____

_____

_____

_____

TELL ME ABOUT IT!

Write a letter to a friend telling about a book you have read. Be sure to include the most important parts of the book in your summary.

_____
(your address)
_____

_____
(date)

_____
(greeting)

_____

_____

_____

_____

_____

_____

_____

_____

_____

_____

_____

_____

_____

_____
(closing)

_____
(signature)

MAKING YOUR

1 WRITING AN OPINION ARTICLE: CHOOSING A TOPIC

Your magazine has been praised by critics for its interesting articles and excellent artwork. Your readers now want to know your opinion about important questions. Before you can give them an answer, you have to be sure about how you feel. To figure out your viewpoint, follow these steps.

• Think about the theme of your magazine. What are some ideas about it that are important to you? Brainstorm a list of questions about your theme on your Idea Pad. Now choose the one question that interests you the most. Write it here.

_____

• Now make a list of pros and cons (points for and points against). In each list, write arguments that support that viewpoint.

Pro	Con
_____	_____
_____	_____
_____	_____

Which list, Pro or Con, seems to you to have better arguments? The answer to that question tells you the viewpoint you want to defend in your article.

2 DRAFTING AND REVISING YOUR OPINION ARTICLE

One good way to write an opinion article is to predict the arguments someone might express and then answer those arguments one by one. This is where a Pro and Con list can come in handy. You have already listed both sides of the argument.

When you are ready to edit and revise, put yourself in the place of a reader who disagrees. Are your arguments convincing enough to change that reader's mind?

IDEA PAD

Ready to publish your opinion article? Turn to page 128.

OWN MAGAZINE

1 Planning an Opinion Poll

A

My dog is a good friend.

I like to take her to the park.

My dog is loyal.

What do you like most about having a dog?

We play catch.

My dog protects me.

He warns me of danger.

After your opinion article appeared in the magazine, many readers wrote in. Some agreed with you, and others did not. You decide to take a poll among your classmates to see what they think and to publish the results in a chart or graph.

How do you go about taking an opinion poll? One way is to ask questions and let people answer any way they want. The problem with this method is that presenting the answers in a chart would be difficult, since all answers would be different. See Box A.

Another way is to make statements and ask people how much they agree or disagree. This way it is easier to create a chart, since you control the possible answers. See Box B.

Write some questions or statements for your poll:

_____

_____

_____

_____

B

disagree slightly   disagree   disagree strongly

The best reason to have a dog is for protection.

agree slightly   agree   agree strongly

2 TAKING THE POLL

Ask many people your questions. Keep track of their answers in a notebook.

Now plan how you will show the information. Here are two kinds of graphs. Choose one of these, or design your own chart.

Ready for the next steps? Turn to page 129.

MY MAGAZINE

disagree strongly • agree slightly • agree • agree strongly • disagree slightly • disagree

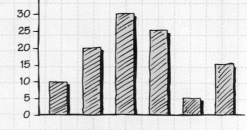

30 25 20 15 10 5 0

Read about "Yesteryear."
Then turn to page 42.

Now Hair This!

Why do lawyers and judges in England wear white wigs?

The English lawyer's wig is a style left over from 300 years ago. At that time all important men in England wore wigs. The wigs had long curls that came down over the men's shoulders. Wig styles changed around the year 1700. The new style had hair pulled back in a ponytail. But lawyers and judges kept the older-style wigs as a sign of the importance of the law.

In the 1790s it was the style for men to put powder on their wigs. Some wigs were powdered white. Other wigs were light pink, silver, or blue!

Is it true that George Washington wore a wig?

No. People often say he did because wigs were in style for important men at the time of the American Revolution. Although many of the men who founded the United States wore wigs, Washington always wore only his own hair. He powdered it and pulled it back in a ponytail.

from CHARLIE BROWN'S FOURTH SUPER BOOK OF QUESTIONS AND ANSWERS: ABOUT ALL KINDS OF PEOPLE AND HOW THEY LIVE!
Charles M. Schulz

Benjamin Banneker made the first clock assembled in the United States. It was made from wood and ran for 20 years!

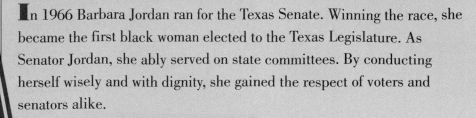

Leading the Way

In 1966 Barbara Jordan ran for the Texas Senate. Winning the race, she became the first black woman elected to the Texas Legislature. As Senator Jordan, she ably served on state committees. By conducting herself wisely and with dignity, she gained the respect of voters and senators alike.

In fall of 1972, Texas elected Barbara Jordan to the United States House of Representatives. She moved to Washington, D.C., and became the first black woman from the South to be a member of Congress.

from *Twenty Texans* by Betsy Warren

FIRST LADY UNDER FIRE

During the War of 1812 British troops attacked Washington, D.C. Just a few hours before the soldiers arrived to burn the President's house, First Lady Dolly Madison wrote in a letter to her sister:

3 o'clock Will you believe it, my sister? We have had a battle or skirmish near Bladensburg, and I am still here, within sound of the cannon!…Our kind friend Mr. Carroll has come to hasten my departure and is in a very bad humor with me because I insist on waiting until the large picture of General Washington is secured, and it requires to be unscrewed from the wall. This process was found too tedious for those perilous moments. I have ordered the frame to be broken and the canvas taken out. It is done—and the precious portrait placed in the hands of two gentlemen from New York for safekeeping.

from *Dolly Madison* by Katharine Anthony

Do one of these:

If you could talk with someone who lived long ago, who would it be? Tell why you would choose that person. Then make a list of questions you would ask the person.

Imagine that you are living in another time period. Write a paragraph telling what you think your life would have been like if you had lived then.

by_____

(your name)

Attean showed Matt how to make a bow and arrows out of found objects. Think of something you can make out of natural things or trash. Try to make it from 100% natural or discarded things. Can you make your own string, glue, or staples if you need them? Write a description of your project below.

THE ART OF Creation

What I'll make _CATWHATWOBWLWONTUTAIWN_

Materials _LOSNBRWWWOWTIN_

How to Make It _J OCELYNN LILLYEN_

Plans made by _____
                          (your name)

LIGHT of my LIFE

What is precious to you? Who or what do you cherish seeing or hearing every day? Write a poem about someone or something that you treasure.

Title_____

by_____

(your name)

American Flags

"The American Revolution: A Picture Sourcebook" gave you some background information about the people, events, and flags of the American Revolution. Imagine that you are a patriot in Revolutionary War times. Design a different flag for the Americans. Draw your flag in the space. Then write about your design, telling what the colors and symbols mean.

design by _____
(your name)

★ ★ ★ ★ ★ ★ ★ ★ ★ ★ ★ ★ ★

Geordie and his mother are glad that Will is safely home, but Father has promised to treat Will as a traitor. If you were Geordie, what would you say to your father to persuade him to welcome Will back? In the space below, write your most persuasive argument.

A Little Persuasion

_____
(your name)

What rules and procedures must the students in your classroom follow? Make a poster that lists the rules in your own words. Paraphrase the rules to help new students understand the information.

CLASSROOM RULES

Paraphrased by_____

(your name)

Elizabeth Answers

by _____
(your name)

You read about a young woman's ambition in "Elizabeth Blackwell." Write what you think Elizabeth would have said in response to each of these statements.

Only men should be doctors!

There are not many jobs that women can do.

You should disguise yourself as a man so you can attend medical lectures.

PLANNING FOR A VISIT

Choose one of the prominent women you read about and imagine that she is visiting your school. Fill in the planning sheets for her visit.

Name of the Visitor _____

Places to Show the Visitor _____

_____

_____

_____

_____

_____

_____

_____

_____

_____

_____

Facts About Your School to Share with the Visitor _____

_____

_____

_____

_____

_____

_____

_____

_____

Questions to Ask When Interviewing the Visitor _____

_____

_____

_____

_____

Planning Sheets by

_____
(your name)

STAND UP AND BE COUNTED

Lila thinks it is important that women vote. In the space below, write a speech for Lila. Be sure to have Lila tell why she believes as she does and what action she wants her listeners to take.

_____

_____

_____

_____

_____

_____

_____

_____

_____

_____

_____

_____

_____

_____

_____

_____

_____

_____

speech writer: _____
                        (your name)

DO YOU AGREE ?

"I think we students should be allowed to choose which subjects to study in fifth grade," Marcus said.

Do you agree or disagree? Write a paragraph that will persuade your readers that your opinion is the correct one. Be sure to use persuasion to guide readers to believe as you do.

ABCD EFGHIJKLMNOPQRS
TUVWXYS

Signed, _____
(your name)

Stories

Thomas has a special interest in the Civil War and the Underground Railroad. What part of American history is most interesting to you? Write a few paragraphs telling what event or time period in America's past interests you most, how you became interested in it, and why.

of the Past

written by

_____

(your name)

Let's Celebrate

You read about a holiday celebration of the past in "The Bells of Christmas." Now, imagine that you are living one hundred years in the future. How do you think holidays will be celebrated then? Write a description of a holiday celebration a hundred years from now.

HAPPY HOLIDAYS!

GREETINGS....GR

description by _____

(your name)

MAKING YOUR

1 WRITING A STORY

You know your readers like stories, so you'll include a story in your magazine. Four pages are set aside for your fiction story.

Your story may be based on a true experience. Search your own memory for a good story. Ask yourself questions such as: **What was the best day in my life? What happy, sad, frightening, or exciting experience have I had that would make a good story?** Write some of these experiences on your Idea Pad.

You can also look in a newspaper or a news magazine for story ideas. As you read the news stories, ask yourself questions like these: **How did that hero feel? What will become of that child? What went on before the big game?** Write some story ideas from the news on your Idea Pad.

Now look over the ideas you have listed. Choose the one that would make the best story. Write it here: _____

_____

IDEA PAD

_____
_____
_____
_____
_____
_____
_____
_____
_____
_____
_____
_____
_____
_____
_____
_____

If your point of view is omniscient, you know everything. As the storyteller, you know what all the characters are thinking.

2 Choosing a Point of View

Now that you have chosen a story idea, the next step is to choose a point of view. Will you tell the story as if it is happening to you (limited point of view)? Would it be better to tell the story as if you are watching it happen to someone else (omniscient point of view)?

Write your point of view here:

_____

_____

If your point of view is limited, you know the thoughts of only one character.

OWN MAGAZINE

3 PLANNING YOUR STORY

Before you begin writing, you must have a plan. To get started, think for a moment about your main character. Close your eyes and picture this character. What does he or she look like? What is his or her personality like?

Jot down some ideas about your character on the first line below.

What will happen in your story? Think about how your character would act in certain situations. Jot down a few things that will happen to

the character and a few things that the character will cause to happen.

How will your story end? Even though you may not be sure at this point, you can jot down a few ideas in the third column.

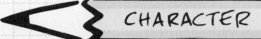

CHARACTER   PLOT   ENDING

_____   _____   _____

_____   _____   _____

_____   _____   _____

_____   _____   _____

You can write from the first-person point of view, even if the story you are telling is not your own. Just put yourself in the other person's place, and use the pronoun I as that person would.

You can write from the third-person point of view, even if the story you are telling is about yourself. Just imagine that you are watching yourself, and use <u>he</u> or <u>she</u> as you describe your own activities and thoughts.

Will you add illustrations? Use as many or as few as you wish. Draw them, or cut pictures from magazines and newspapers.

MY MAGAZINE

Ready to publish? See pages 130-133.

4 DRAFTING AND REVISING

Now it's time to experiment with your ideas. Let them flow quickly for your first draft. Sometimes your thoughts get ahead of your pencil, and you must hurry to keep up!

When you are finished with your first draft, read it with a critic's eye. Put yourself in the place of the reader. Do you feel that the characters would have acted that way in real life? If not, change what they do. Read your story to a classmate. Work together to improve it.

Read all about "Shenanigans."
Then turn to page 60.

Accidentally

Once — I didn't mean to,
but that
was that —
I yawned in the sunshine
and swallowed a gnat.
I'd rather eat mushrooms
and bullfrogs' legs,
I'd rather have pepper
all over my eggs
than open my mouth
on a sleepy day
and close on a gnat
going down that way.
It tasted sort of salty.
It didn't hurt a bit.
I accidentally ate a gnat,
and that
was
it!

by Maxine W. Kumin

The Rooster's Song

The Rooster's song flew through the air
like a silver arrow.

I blow a trumpet of gold,
I wear a crimson hat,
And with my reveille bold
I wake up the Dog and the Cat.
The day has begun to unfold,
So the Snake and the Bird and the Rat
And you, Cocori, are told:
Rise and shine! And good night to the Bat.

from *Cocori* by Joaquín Gutiérrez

Young Mozart

Born in 1756, Wolfgang Amadeus Mozart learned to play the clavier (an early keyboard instrument) at the age of three and wrote his first concerto when he was five. In a few years the remarkable child was playing for the royal families of Europe.

Wolfgang's success at court was such that Mr. Mozart decided his son should play for the general public. The boy gave his first subscription concert on June 5, 1764. Everyone praised him.

However, Wolfgang was still a little boy. One day when he was playing at a party, a kitten crossed the room. Wolfgang suddenly stopped playing, jumped from his chair, and ran to the kitten. His father had a hard time bringing him back to the keyboard.

from *Mozart: Music Magician* by Claire Huchet Bishop

THE MOON IN FACT

The force of gravity on the moon is only one-sixth that of the earth.

The moon affects the earth's gravity, pulling the water in the oceans away from the earth, causing the twice-daily tides.

Because of its small mass and low gravity, the moon cannot retain even a thin atmosphere; there is no sound on the moon, since sound waves need gas through which to travel. There is also very little light on this airless, waterless world.

Without a blanketing atmosphere, there is a great contrast between day and night temperatures on the moon. Lunar noon is a boiling 212° F., while at lunar midnight, the temperature drops to −24° F.

from *The Second Kids' World Almanac of Records and Facts*
by Margo McLoone-Basta and Alice Siegel

WRITE ABOUT SHENANIGANS

Do one of these:

Imagine that you are a firefly or other type of insect. What dangers would you have to watch out for? Write a dialogue between your character and an older insect character. The older character is saying "be careful" and warning about things such as humans and larger animals. How would your character answer?

Imagine that you are chosen to design a domed city on the moon! Draw and label your design; then present it to your classmates.

by _____

(your name)

WORD PICTURES

"Fireflies" paints a vivid word picture of the flickering flight of fireflies. Think about another insect or animal you have seen. Fill in the word web about the insect or animal you have chosen.

WORDS THAT DESCRIBE THE ANIMAL OR INSECT

WORDS THAT DESCRIBE ITS MOVEMENT

NAME OF THE ANIMAL OR INSECT

_____

by _____
(your name)

WORDS THAT DESCRIBE YOUR FEELINGS WHEN YOU WATCH THE ANIMAL OR INSECT

PHRASES THAT COMPARE IT TO SOMETHING ELSE

A SPIDER HAS FEELINGS, TOO

Jake is terrified when the wolf spider crawls down his back in "Like Jake and Me." If you had been the spider, what would you have thought about Jake's reaction? What would you have done? Rewrite from the spider's point of view the story of Jake and Alex's search for the fuzzy creature.

_____

(your name)

A Jumping-Off Place

Think of a time when you or a friend were frightened by something. What happened? What feelings did you or your friend have? How did you or your friend react? Think about how you could use that real-life incident as a jumping-off place for an exciting imaginary story. Use the space below to plan a story you might write.

_____
(title)

by _____
(your name)

The real-life incident _____

_____

How I felt _____

_____

_____

What I did _____

_____

_____

_____

How I could stretch the truth to make the incident sound more exciting (Perhaps a different setting, unusual characters, or complications?) _____

_____

_____

JUST ALIKE? NOT QUITE!

Think of two objects or animals that seem very different from each other. Can you find ways that the two are alike? Write a descriptive paragraph pointing out ways in which the two are alike and different. Be sure to include interesting and humorous details to help readers compare and contrast.

_____
(your name)

BUG FOOD

If you were Andy, how would you persuade your family and friends that you were right? In the space below, design and write a poster that points out the benefits of eating beetles, bugs, and worms.

created by _____
(your name)

NIGHT PICTURES

_____
_____
_____
_____
_____
_____
_____
_____
_____
_____
_____
_____

by_____
(your name)

_____
_____
_____
_____
_____
_____
_____
_____
_____
_____
_____
_____
_____
_____
_____

"Moon" uses
descriptive words
and images to tell
how the moon looked
to the poet. Picture in
your mind what you
would see if you were
going home late at night.
Write sentences that
would help a reader
see the picture
in your mind.

WISH LIST

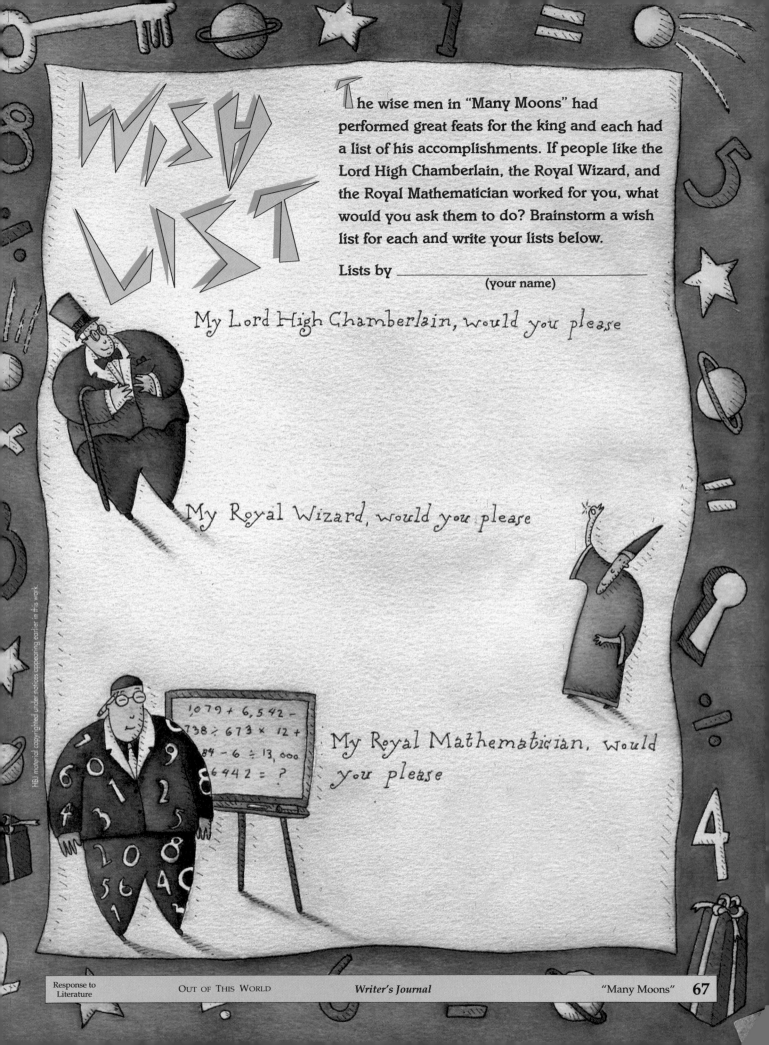

The wise men in "Many Moons" had performed great feats for the king and each had a list of his accomplishments. If people like the Lord High Chamberlain, the Royal Wizard, and the Royal Mathematician worked for you, what would you ask them to do? Brainstorm a wish list for each and write your lists below.

Lists by _____
(your name)

My Lord High Chamberlain, would you please

My Royal Wizard, would you please

My Royal Mathematician, would you please

The MOST AMAZING ACT in the UNIVERSE!

What's your favorite circus act? Pretend that you are the ringmaster and you want to focus the attention of the audience on the next act. What will you say when you announce and describe the act? Write the ringmaster's introduction below. Remember to include figurative language to help readers and listeners visualize the act.

LADIES AND GENTLEMEN!

Ringmaster: _____
(your name)

Dear Advice Column,

I have a neighbor named Oliver Hyde who lives a terribly lonely life. I want to get him out of the house and enjoying life again.

What suggestions do you have to help me help Oliver?

Dear Oliver's Neighbor,

Imagine that you write an advice column in the newspaper and you receive this letter. How do you respond?

Sincerely,

_____
(your name)

LIGHTS, CAMERA, ACTION!

Think about a talent show you'd like to be in. What would you do for a performance? Write about your special talents and what you would do in a school talent show.

_____
_____
_____
_____
_____
_____
_____
_____
_____
_____
_____
_____
_____
_____
_____
_____

NEXT ACT

_____
(your name)

PERFORMING

MAKING YOUR

IDEA PAD

_____

_____

_____

_____

_____

_____

_____

1 Choosing a Topic for a How-To Article

You have two pages in your magazine to include a project that you think readers might enjoy doing. To choose a project, think about the theme of your magazine. List some possible projects on your Idea Pad. Then look over your list and choose the most interesting one. Write it here:

_____

_____

2 LISTING SUPPLIES

When writing directions, you should first list the supplies that are needed. In the box below, write what is needed for your project. You can add to the list later if necessary.

3 INCLUDING SAFETY TIPS

It's always a good idea to warn your reader about any danger involved. For example, if your directions are for having a barbecue, you should include a safety warning about lighting the fire.

4 Writing in Step-by-Step Order

What's the first step in the project? What's the second? Be sure to write your directions in order. Write a first draft, including all the steps.

5 Revising

Give your first draft to a classmate who has never done your project before. If he or she can follow the directions, then you've probably included all the steps. Check over your wording. Is everything clear? If not, fix it.

6 Illustrating

Pictures can be very helpful with directions. You might want to use a picture for each step.

Ready to publish? See pages 134-135.

OWN MAGAZINE

1. Planning Letters of Advice

You've been getting lots of letters asking for advice. Some of these letters come from children, and some come from parents. You'll answer two of them in this issue of your magazine. Turn to pages 136–137 to take a look at the space set aside for your advice columns.

Advice to a Child from a Parent

For this column, imagine you are a parent receiving a letter from a child asking for advice. You will write both parts—the letter and the answer. Think about the kinds of advice a child might want from a parent. Brainstorm a list of ideas on your Idea Pad. Circle the most interesting one.

Advice to a Parent from a Child

For this column, you are a child who has received a letter from a parent asking for advice. You will write the letter and the answer. Think about the kinds of advice a parent might want from a child. Brainstorm a list of ideas on your Idea Pad. Circle the most interesting one.

How can we make meals more enjoyable?

What can my child and I do together on a Saturday?

Should children be paid for doing chores?

What can I do to earn some money?

What's a good book to read?

How do you use this socket wrench?

How can I get along better with my siblings?

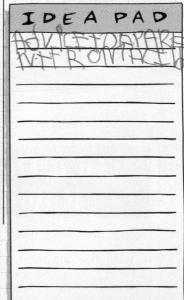

IDEA PAD

2. Writing Letters of Advice

Now that you've decided on a question for each column, brainstorm a list of answers for each one. Be serious or silly, as you prefer, but always be creative.

Write drafts of your letters and the answers. Be sure that your advice answers the question. Read your letters and the answers to a classmate. Work together to improve them.

MY MAGAZINE

Ready to publish? See pages 136-137.

5

UNIT FIVE — LIFELINES

Read about "Lifelines."
Then turn to page 76.

Going... Going...

The Asian elephant once ranged across southern Asia from the Middle East to Vietnam and south to Malaya. It was hunted for its ivory tusks and it is restricted to small areas. Its numbers are decreasing.

The California condor is one of the rarest birds in the world. Some of the last remaining birds have been captured and are being bred in captivity, for eventual release into the wild. Its habitat has been destroyed.

The gharial is a fish-eating crocodile from India, which came close to extinction. It was saved by removing and artificially incubating its eggs. The young gharials were then released into protected areas.

from Close to Extinction
by John Burton

In a Double Rainbow

in a double rainbow
lives the summer rain
who brings the seed
to soak the ground
to make dry arroyos run
as singing summer floods

by Harold Littlebird

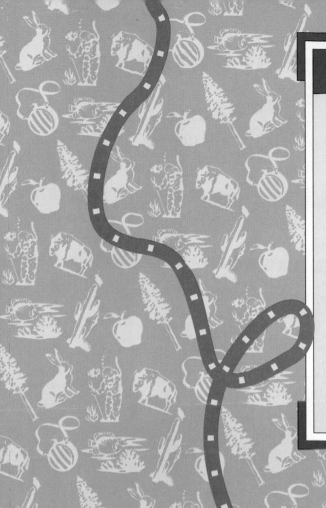

Trees Help Fight Pollution

City air is dirty air. Think about all the cars, trucks, and buses in a city. Think about all the factories and incinerators that put dirt and gases into the air. Air pollution hurts trees as well as people. But trees also help protect us from the dirt and gases in the air. Trees help make the air a little cleaner. How do they do this?

Leaves on trees catch some of the dirt in the air. When it rains, the dirt is washed off the leaves and returned to the ground. And remember that trees are putting fresh oxygen into the air every day. They do this through their leaves, too.

from It's Your Environment: Things to Think About—Things to Do,
edited by Sherry Koehler

DESERT TRAVELER

Living on the desert, Arabian, or one-humped, camels often must travel long distances without eating or drinking. They can travel more than 600 miles (966 km) without a sip of water. They feed on desert plants that provide much of the moisture they need. Many desert plants have thorns. Camels' mouths, however, are tough enough to manage even the thorniest plants.

When camels reach water, they may drink great quantities—until their bellies bulge. A camel may drink as much as 30 gallons (114 L) at one time.

from SECRETS OF ANIMAL SURVIVAL
published by the National Geographic Society

WRITE ABOUT **LIFELINES**

Do one of these:

Plan a perfect planet! What plants and animals would live on your perfect planet? List the ones you would choose, and tell why you chose each one.

Get others to help care for the environment! Design a billboard that will persuade others to help save the wildlife in your area.

by _____
(your name)

DESERT DAY

Think about the description of the desert that you read. Write a diary entry describing a July day in the desert.

_____ 's Diary
(your name)

_____

Daybreak: _____

_____

_____

_____

8:00 A.M. _____

_____

_____

_____

Noon: _____

_____

_____

_____

4:00 P.M. _____

_____

_____

_____

Sunset: _____

_____

CHASE

"Jackrabbit" uses the rabbit's point of view to describe its escape from a coyote. Write a poem describing the same chase from the coyote's point of view. Give your poem a title.

written by _____
(your name)

_____

_____

_____

_____

_____

_____

_____

_____

_____

_____

_____

Pretend that you are a scientist studying the life cycle of the monarch that begins when a monarch butterfly lays her eggs. Lucky to find the eggs shortly after they have been laid, you decide to keep a journal of what you see. Though you are fascinated, you know that as a scientist, you must write down only what you see. (You can use a microscope if you like.) Be clear and specific in your writing.

OBSERVER'S JOURNAL

Observer: _____
(your name)

Thing Observed: Life cycle of the monarch butterfly

Habitat:

A few days after the eggs were laid,

After two weeks of eating,

Once it stops eating,

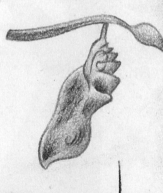

After fifteen days in the chrysalis,

An hour after emerging from the chrysalis,

WAITING FOR...

The time just before a new season can be exciting because everybody is expecting something. That makes it a great setting for a story! Think of a time of year when everyone is waiting for something to happen. The coming of baseball season? The end of a heat wave? Describe that time of year, and the waiting that comes with it, in what could be the opening paragraphs of a story.

_____

(story title)

_____

(your name)

_____
_____
_____
_____
_____
_____
_____
_____
_____
_____
_____
_____
_____

Today's Forecast

You are the weather forecaster for central Vermont. It is mid-March. You know everyone is waiting for good news, but all you can predict is more of the same harsh weather. Prepare an honest but comforting opening statement in the box below. Tell your audience what kind of weather to expect tomorrow.

Tomorrow's Weather

_____

_____

_____

Next, list some facts that support your statement. _____

_____

_____

_____

Now write your weather report. Let your opening statement express the main idea—the kind of weather to expect tomorrow. Then support it with specific details.

_____

_____

_____

_____

_____

_____ , **Weather Forecaster**

_____
(your name)

You Can Do It, Too!

Think about something you can do well. How would you teach someone else to do it? Write a paragraph that will explain, step by step, how to do it. Keep your directions clear and in correct order.

How to --

by --

(your name)

SAVANNAH SCENE

These animals live on the African savannah. What do you think is happening in the drawing below? Write a story to go with the picture.

written by _____
(your name)

HERE'S A STORY

STORY IDEAS

BY _____

(YOUR NAME)

Tall tales have been written about the man described in "Johnny Appleseed." Think about Johnny's journey on foot across the country. What adventures can you imagine that he might have had? Make a list of story ideas about a character who walks across the United States.

TELL IT TALL

Make up a tall tale of your own, and write it in the space below. You might tell how your favorite tree or flower came to be.

_____

_____

_____

_____

_____

_____

_____

_____

_____

_____

_____

_____

_____

written by _____
                          (your name)

Read the story beginning and ending below. Then plan a middle for the story. Make a list of the events and details you will include. Remember to provide details that readers can draw on to make generalizations about the story characters and events.

ON THE TRAIL

Sarah plodded slowly beside the oxen that pulled her family's covered wagon. It was hot on the plains in midsummer, but every step took the family closer to their new home in Oregon. Sarah's little brother Dan lagged a few steps behind, his small face still streaked with the tears that had fallen often during the last two days, ever since his dog Prince had wandered away from the wagon train and disappeared.

Events and details for the middle of the story:

Sarah patted the dog's rough fur. "Isn't that just like old Prince to turn up when we needed him most?" Prince cocked his head. Sarah was sure he was smiling.

by _____
(your name)

MAKING YOUR ®

1 Planning the Poet's Corner

1 Your magazine includes a section devoted to poetry. You publish some poems from your readers, and you add a few of your own. You often include artwork with the poetry. Turn to page 138 to see the space reserved for the "Poet's Corner."

What kind of poetry will you put on this page? Will it rhyme or not? Will the lines have repeating patterns or rhythm—a certain beat? Will the subjects be serious or funny? Will the poems be long or short? Think about topics that apply to the themes of your magazine. Write a list of poem topics. Circle your favorites, and cross out the others.

2 WRITING SOME POEMS

2 Now play with these topics by writing lines of poetry. Get help from a classmate. Work together to write some interesting poems.

Choose the best poems to include in your magazine. If you wish, use watercolors, markers, chalk, or pencil to create pictures to go with the poems. You may want to cut pictures from magazines or create collages from art scraps. It's up to you.

Ready to publish? See page 138 for the next steps.

REMEMBER!

Write a list of poem topics:

A haiku is a three-line poem:
first line = five syllables,
second line = seven syllables,
third line = five syllables.

A CONCRETE POEM
SUBJECT
IS IN
THE SHAPE OF ITS

A lyric poem is about personal feelings or experiences.

A narrative poem tells a story.

OWN MAGAZINE

1 PLANNING AN INTERVIEW WITH THE POET

This issue will include an interview with a poet. Choose one of the poems you wrote for your Poet's Corner. Imagine it was written by someone else and you have a chance to interview that poet. Plan your interview by writing a list of questions.

List your questions here:

_____

_____

_____

_____

_____

What inspired you to write this poem?

Do you make a living as a poet, or do you have another job?

For how long have you been writing poetry?

What were you trying to achieve in this poem?

What other kinds of poems do you like to write?

2 Conducting the Interview

Remember that you are the poet as well as the interviewer. You'll be answering all those questions yourself! Write answers to your questions.

3 Drafting and Revising the Article

How will you turn these questions and answers into an article? Here are some ideas:

- Write them as a series of questions and answers.
- Make them into a story about the interview.
- Make them into a news article about the poet. Include the five Ws (who, what, when, where, why).

Choose one of these ideas, or think of your own. Write a first draft. Show your draft to a classmate. Work together to improve weak sentences, fix any spelling errors, and correct the punctuation.

Don't forget to add illustrations and captions.

Ready to publish? See page 139 for the next steps.

Read about "Flights."
Then turn to page 92.

UNIT SIX
FLIGHTS

Airborne Animals

Nobody knows how many birds there are in the world. Scientists who study these airborne animals say there may be as many as 100 billion.

The great horned owl can turn its head almost all the way around. An owl can do this because it has 14 neck bones—twice as many as humans have. An owl cannot move its eyes. Instead, it moves its whole head.

A pileated woodpecker has a thick skull. It helps protect the brain while the woodpecker hammers at trees. The pileated woodpecker chips away wood to uncover insects that bore into trees. It also pecks out holes for nests.

By beating its wings very fast, the hummingbird can stay in one spot in the air. It also can take off straight upward or fly sideways. It can even fly backward—and it is the only bird that can do this! A hummingbird's wings beat as fast as 100 times a second. To the human eye, they appear as a blur. The humming sound of the wings led to the bird's name. Some humming-birds are less than an inch long.

from *Far-Out Facts*
published by the National Geographic Society

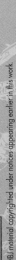

Time with a Capital T

I've read some of the stuff about Time with a capital T, and I don't say I understand it too well. But I know Einstein or somebody compares Time to a winding river, and says we exist as though in a boat, drifting along between high banks. All we can see is the present, immediately around us. We can't see the future just beyond the next curve, or the past in the many bends in back of us. But it's all there just the same. There—countless bends back, in infinite distance—lies the past, as real as the moment around us.

from ABOUT TIME by Jack Finney

Just Plane Safe

People can wear parachutes, so why can't planes? Actually, they can.

The idea, it is said, came about by accident in the early 1900s. As a pilot was jumping from his disabled plane, his parachute lines got tangled in the craft. The chute opened anyway and floated both pilot and plane to safety.

Recently companies have started making parachutes specially for airplanes. Engineers estimate it would take 24 parachutes, each with enough cloth to cover a football field, to lower a loaded 747.

from *National Geographic World*, October 1990

WRITE ABOUT FLIGHTS

Do one of these:

If you could fly anywhere, where would you go? Write a story about your fantasy flight.

What's your favorite kind of flying machine? Make a poster showing your favorite and telling all about it.

by_____

(your name)

Pretend that your family is going to spend a day in New Providence. What do you want to see? Will the trip be an educational tour or just fun? Consider the interests of each person in your family so that everyone will have something to look forward to see. Make your plans for morning, afternoon, and evening.

PLAN A TRIP!

Itinerary by _____ (your name)

IN THE MORNING

7 AM   For Breakfast _____

10 AM _____

IN THE AFTERNOON

12 PM For Lunch _____

2 PM _____

4 PM _____

AT NIGHT

6 PM For Dinner _____

8 PM _____

The Changing Cityscape

Choose one of the time periods described for New Providence and give your viewpoint of the city for that time. Did you find the changes exciting? Are the signs garish? Is the town square comfortable? What are your feelings about the city? Describe a walk through a part of the city using words that reveal your attitude about particular buildings, the town square, or changes that were made.

by: _____

(your name)

Recipe for Change

Wow! It would really change the story if I put

_____ **in it!**

Story Idea by _____

(your name)

When you add a new character to a story, something's bound to change! Choose a character you know from a book or movie and drop that character into "A Wrinkle in Time." Assume that the first person Meg, Calvin, and Charles Wallace meet at Central Central is the character you have selected. Who is it? Sherlock Holmes? Alice from Wonderland? Captain Hook? Sally Ride? Choose your character and write the beginning paragraph of the next episode of the story.

The Next CHAPTER

"Buck Rogers in the 25th Century" tells about the beginning of Buck's trip to Mars. What do you think happened when he finally reached Mars? Write and draw the next installment of the comic strip in the panels below.

Buck Rogers

written by: _____
(your name)

HBJ material copyrighted under notices appearing earlier in this work.

A DAY IN SPACE

If you went along on a space flight like the one Sally Ride describes in "To Space & Back," what would be your favorite part of the trip? Write an entry for your log book, telling about that part of your journey.

_____'s Log Book

Date: _____

Wish You Were Here!

Dear _____

_____

_____

_____

_____

_____

_____

_____

_____

_____
(your name)

Dear _____

_____

_____

_____

_____

_____

_____

_____

_____

_____
(your name)

What you write in a log book would be different from what you would write in a postcard to a friend or a relative. Take the information you wrote in your log book and use it to compose postcards to people back home. Write one postcard to a young friend and another to an older relative. What might you write about to each person?

If you could have any animal for a pet, what would you choose? You could write a paragraph of realistic fiction or fantasy about your choice, or you might write a nonfiction journal entry or informational article about it. Choose a type of fiction or nonfiction, and write a paragraph about the pet you would like to have.

A Fine Pet

by _____

(your name)

SPACE QUESTIONS

"Secrets" points out how little we know about space. What are some things you wish you knew? In each planet, write a question about space you would like to have answered.

by _____
(your name)

Just imagine moving to a new planet, as the characters do in "The Green Book." If you were the Guide, what would you have the families do to begin the settlement on the new planet? Write your instructions to them.

GUIDELINES

On the first day:

Later in the first week:

Later in the first month:

Guide: _____

(your name)

THE VIEW FROM HERE!

Think about the scene when Patti and the other Earth people arrive on a new planet and name it Shine. How might this scene change if told by a being who is already living on that planet?

Make up a name for such a being, and have him, her, or it write a report describing the arrival of a spaceship and the strange beings that emerge from it.

Report by: _____

Date: _____

MAKING YOUR

Creating the Career Page

Your readers are looking forward to your Career of the Month page. Think about your magazine's theme. What jobs might go with that theme? See the box for some examples.

Now you try it. What's your magazine about? What careers could go with it? Brainstorm a list of them. From this list, choose the career that appeals to you most. Ask yourself, "What kind of person—shy, friendly, athletic, careful—would enjoy such a job? How would someone prepare for this career? What would a typical day on the job be like? Would any of the work be boring?"

Use the answers to these questions to create your Career of the Month page. Don't forget to add illustrations.

A reader of a magazine about animal rights might . . .

- be a vet
- be a pet-sitter
- work in a zoo
- write books about animals
- sell pet equipment
- be a judge at pet shows

Ready?
Go to page 140.

Creating the HELP-WANTED Section

Your magazine has a help-wanted section. Turn to page 141 to take a look. Imagine the page covered with ads.

Your ads should appeal to your readers. If you wanted help building a house, you wouldn't advertise in a knitting magazine, would you? Remember the theme of your magazine before you write your ads.

For ideas, look at the classified section of a newspaper or a magazine. Notice that these ads are very short and use many abbreviations. They also include a telephone number—and sometimes a name. Be creative. Make some ads funny and some serious. Make all of them interesting.

Ready to publish your page of ads?
Go to page 141.

OWN MAGAZINE

Putting Together a Puzzle Page

Ready to create a puzzle page? See page 142.

Your readers have sent letters praising the puzzle page in your magazine. You want to keep them happy by publishing another perplexing puzzle. What will it be this time? A crossword? Some riddles? A map with some clues to hidden treasure? Maybe you'd like to print a game board and include directions so your readers can play a game on it.

Have a brainstorming session with a classmate to answer this question: What kinds of puzzles or games would be fun for your magazine? Think about puzzles you've worked on and games you've played. Can you invent one to go along with the theme of your magazine? After you've created your puzzle or game, play it to make sure it works. Revise it as necessary.

Ready to create your vocabulary page? See page 143.

WRITING A VOCABULARY PAGE

Page 143 of your magazine is set aside for funny vocabulary. Make up some words that sound as if they would go with the theme of your magazine. Add some daffy definitions to go with the words. Have your readers match up the definitions and the words.

Supply an answer key and scoring guide. For example:

7–8 correct = superstar
5–6 correct = star
3–4 correct = OK
1–2 correct = are you awake?

FINISHING UP YOUR MAGAZINE

You are almost finished with your magazine. There are just a few things left to do:

- **Complete the Table of Contents.**
  Turn to page 122 in your magazine. Write your title for each writing project in the Table of Contents.
- **Design the back cover of your magazine.**
  Turn to page 144. Find pictures from newspapers or magazines or draw your own to create your back cover.
- **Take a final look through your magazine.**
  Look for places where you could improve it. Put the finishing touches on your pages.

Go to page 122 to find the Table of Contents.

Acknowledgments

Text Selections

For permission to reprint copyrighted material, grateful acknowledgment is made to the following sources:

Aladdin Books Ltd.: From pp. 30, 31 in *Close to Extinction* (Retitled: "Going . . . Going . . .") by John Burton. Text © 1988 by Aladdin Books Ltd.

Curtis Brown, Ltd.: "Accidentally" from *No One Writes a Letter to a Snail* by Maxine W. Kumin. Text copyright © 1962 by Maxine W. Kumin. Published by G. P. Putnam's Sons.

Cormorant Books Ltd.: "A Boy Fulfills His Promise" (Retitled: "The Rooster's Song") from *Cocori* by Joaquín Gutiérrez, translated by Daniel McBain. Text copyright © 1989 by Joaquín Gutiérrez; translation copyright © 1989 by Daniel McBain.

Doubleday, a division of Bantam Doubleday Dell Publishing Group, Inc.: From *Dolly Madison* (Retitled: "First Lady Under Fire") by Katharine Anthony.

The Environmental Action Coalition: "Trees Help Fight Pollution" from *It's Your Environment: Things to Think About— Things to Do*, edited by Sherry Koehler. Text copyright © 1976, 1975, 1974, 1973, 1972, 1971 by The Environmental Action Coalition, Inc. Published by Charles Scribner's Sons.

Farrar, Straus & Giroux, Inc.: From pp. 16–17 in *The Green Book* by Jill Paton Walsh. Text copyright © 1982 by Jill Paton Walsh.

Funk & Wagnalls Corporation: From "The Moon" (Retitled: "The Moon in Fact") in *The Second Kids' World Almanac of Records and Facts* by Margo McLoone-Basta and Alice Siegel. Text copyright © 1987 by Margo-Alice.

Harcourt Brace & Company: Riddle Poem #2 from *When I Dance* by James Berry. Text copyright © 1991, 1988 by James Berry.

National Geographic Society: From "Airborne Animals" in *Far-Out Facts*. Text copyright © 1980 by National Geographic Society. From "Desert Traveler" in *Secrets of Animal Survival*. Text copyright © 1983 by National Geographic Society.

Random House, Inc.: From pp. 19, 20 in *Charlie Brown's Fourth Super Book of Questions and Answers* by Charles M. Schulz. Text copyright © 1979 by United Feature Syndicate.

Kenneth Rosen: "In a Double Rainbow" by Harold Littlebird from *Voices of the Rainbow: Contemporary Poetry by American Indians*, edited by Kenneth Rosen. Published by The Viking Press (A Richard Seaver Book), New York, 1975.

Photograph Credits

Harcourt Brace & Company Photo/Debi Harbin 27; Warren Faidley/International Stock Photography Ltd. 30; Harcourt Brace & Company Photo/Les Stone 37; H. Armstrong Roberts 52, top left; H. Armstrong Roberts 52, top right; Devaney Collection/Superstock 52, bottom left; Superstock 53, top right; Superstock 53, bottom left; Superstock 53, bottom right; Harcourt Brace & Company Photo/Maria Paraskevas 83; Harcourt Brace & Company Photo 120

Robert Dale, Bernard Adnet, Stacey May, Janice Edelman 107-118

Scott Matthews, Janice Edelman 119-144

WRITER'S HANDBOOK

This is your Writer's Handbook. Look through the headings. The Handbook's reminders and examples will help you as you work on your Magazine. You may also want to refer to your Writer's Handbook as you draft, revise, and proofread other compositions.

WRITING SENTENCES

CAPITAL LETTERS AND END PUNCTUATION

Every sentence begins with a capital letter and ends with an end mark.

Use a **period** at the end of a declarative sentence.

There is really no reason why we can't use insects as a source of protein.

Use a **period** at the end of an imperative sentence.

Count the number of seconds between the flash and the thunder.

Use a **question mark** at the end of an interrogative sentence.

Will the innocent be sent to jail and the guilty go free?

Read all about it!

Use an **exclamation point** at the end of an exclamatory sentence.

Begin all important proper nouns with a capital letter.

Names

The names of **people and pets** are proper nouns.

The names of **days of the week**, **months of the year**, and **holidays** are proper nouns.

> On **July 10th** the wounded mountain lion was forced to hunt in the heat of the day.

The names of **particular places and things**, such as bridges, parks, and buildings, are proper nouns.

> Baseball has been extremely popular throughout **Latin America**.

Begin the **title of a person**, such as Miss or Dr., with a capital letter. The titles Mr., Ms., Mrs., and Dr. are abbreviations. Use a period after each of these titles.

Use a capital letter for an **initial** that **takes the place of a name.** Use a period after an initial.

> From the Mixed-up Files of
> **Mrs. Basil E. Frankweiler**

Write the **pronoun I** as a capital letter.

> Caleb thought the story over, and I didn't tell him what I had really thought.

> ME!

COMMAS

Use a comma before the conjunction **and**, **or**, or **but** when it joins two simple sentences in a compound sentence.

Baseball was born in the United States, **but** it has become popular in other countries over the years.

Use commas to separate words or word groups in a series.

I have brought you divining rods, magic wands, and crystal spheres in which to behold the future.

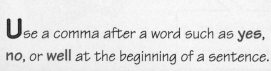

Yes, I do like small rooms sometimes.

Use a comma after a word such as **yes**, **no**, or **well** at the beginning of a sentence.

Person addressed

Use a comma to set off the name of a person or group being directly addressed.

Have they all gone brownish with age, **Dad?**

A direct quotation shows someone's exact words.

DIRECT QUOTATIONS

Use quotation marks before and after a direct quotation.

Begin the first word in a direct quotation with a capital letter.

When other words come before the quotation, use a comma between those words and the first quotation mark.

All of a sudden, he just looked over at me and said, **"I'll take the kid in the red jacket."**

Use another punctuation mark just before the last quotation mark.

When the quotation comes at the end of a sentence, use a **period** if the quotation makes a statement or gives a command or request.

When the quotation does not come at the end of a sentence, use a **comma** if the quotation makes a statement or gives a command or request.

"They can think of no way to hide the moon that will not make the Princess Lenore ill,**"** said the king.

If the quotation asks a question, use a **question mark** before the last quotation mark.

If the quotation is an exclamation, use an **exclamation point** before the last quotation mark.

If the quotation is one sentence divided by words that identify the speaker, use a comma before and after the words that identify the speaker.

Begin the first word, the last word, and each important word in a title with a capital letter.

TITLES

Use quotation marks before and after the title of a story, magazine article, essay, song, or poem. (**"La Bamba"**)

Begin the first word, the last word, and each important word in a title with a capital letter. Underline the title of a book, movie, magazine, or newspaper. (Storms)

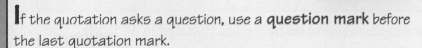

APOSTROPHES

Use an apostrophe in place of the letter or letters that have been left out in a **contraction**.

It's really something, isn't it?

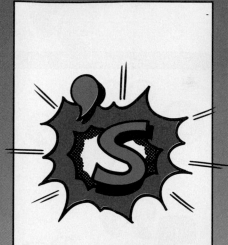

Add an apostrophe and s to most **singular nouns** to show **possession**.

Seemingly oblivious to my fears, Daisy and Buttercup ambled along at a **snail's** pace, despite my shaking the reins to urge them faster.

Add just an apostrophe and s to **plural nouns** that do not end in s to show **possession**.

Today, **women's** opportunities are unlimited, due to the leadership of people such as Elizabeth Blackwell.

Add an apostrophe to **plural nouns** that end in s to show **possession**.

Both nests protect the **birds'** eggs from dangerous snakes.

NEGATIVE WORDS

Negative words are words that mean "no." Some examples are **not, never, nobody, nothing, none,** and **no one.** Use only one negative word to express "no."

SUBJECT-VERB AGREEMENT

Be sure that the present-tense verb in a sentence agrees with the subject of the sentence. **If the subject is singular, add s or es to the verb.**

plural: These **surfaces were** useless in the vacuum of space; but **they become** more effective as the air thickens.

singular: Suddenly, **the ride becomes** very, very smooth and quiet.

CORRECTING RUN-ON SENTENCES

Be sure your writing does not include run-on sentences. A run-on sentence is two or more sentences not separated by correct punctuation or by connecting words.

The World Series was established in 1903. The next year, however, the National League champions refused to play the American League champions.

You can correct a run-on sentence by rewriting it as two simple sentences.

The World Series was established in 1903. but The next year, ~~however,~~ the National League champions refused to play the American League champions.

You can also correct a run-on sentence by adding a comma and the word **and, but** or **or**.

CORRECTING SENTENCE FRAGMENTS

Be sure your writing does not include sentence fragments. A sentence fragment is a group of words that does not have a subject and a predicate. A sentence fragment does not express a complete thought.

You can correct a sentence fragment by adding a subject or a predicate.

Baseball
Probably developed from cricket, a game that has been played in England for more than 700 years. During the 1869-1870 season, the Cincinnati Red Stockings, the first professional baseball team won 91 of their first 92 games.

WRITING PARAGRAPHS

EXPOSITORY PARAGRAPHS

Expository paragraphs give readers information. Begin an expository paragraph with a topic sentence—one sentence that expresses your main idea. Then write other sentences that add information and help readers understand your main idea.

To the African people, the baobab is more than a source of honey. Its bark is stripped for baskets and rope; its fruit is made into candy and sweet drinks; and its roots and leaves are used as medicine. On the hot, dry savannah, the hollow trunks of ancient baobabs can also become water containers and even shelters.

— from "Tree of Life"

NARRATIVE PARAGRAPHS

Narrative paragraphs tell about events. You may use narrative paragraphs when you write stories and when you write about real events. When you write a narrative paragraph, tell about the events in the order they happened. You may want to use time-order words to help you make your paragraph clearer.

When the Museum closed, John Summers went back to his hotel, disappointed his trip was in vain. The following day, he checked out of the hotel at noon. Since his bus did not leave until later that day, Summers locked his black bag, checked it in the hotel's luggage checkroom, and went sightseeing. Later he returned to pick up his bag, and he was promptly arrested.

— from "You Be the Jury"

PERSUASIVE PARAGRAPHS

You write persuasive paragraphs when you want to convince your readers to agree with your opinions. A persuasive paragraph should include a topic sentence—one sentence that expresses your opinion on a topic. Then other sentences in the paragraph should give reasons to support your opinion.

New Providence is thriving. Cobblestone streets bustle with activity—Model T Fords, streetcars, and horse-drawn carts carrying meat, milk, and ice. There is no concert in the bandstand today, but a crowd has gathered in the square in front of the Town Hall and the Tenebo County Courthouse. A fountain has been built in commemoration of Chief Tenebo, a Native American from a local tribe. The statue is about to be unveiled. Around the base of the fountain is an inscription: GOOD CITIZENS ARE THE RICHES OF A CITY.

—from "New Providence: A Changing Cityscape"

DESCRIPTIVE PARAGRAPHS

Descriptive paragraphs describe people, places, things, or events. Begin a descriptive paragraph with a topic sentence—one sentence that identifies what you will describe. Then write other sentences that give details about the person, place, thing, or event you are describing.

Before us lay a wide and gentle plain sloping to the shores of a round wide lake some miles across. Beyond the lake, a very high mountain with perfectly symmetrical slopes rose into the sky, topped with snow. A mirror image of the lovely mountain hung inverted in the lake, quite still, for the surface was like glass, perfectly unruffled by even the slightest impulse of the air.

— from "The Green Book"

WRITING STORIES

INTRODUCTION, DEVELOPMENT, CONCLUSION

When you plan and write a story, think about these three story parts: introduction, development, and conclusion.

In the **introduction**, present the main characters and describe the story setting. Also explain the problem that the main characters must face.

In the middle part of your story, the **development**, tell how the characters try to solve the problem.

In the **conclusion**, tell how the problem is finally solved.

DIALOGUE

You may want to use dialogue to make your story clear and interesting. Remember to begin a new paragraph each time the speaker changes. Use words such as **whispered**, **answered**, or **shouted** to show how the speaker says the words.

"You don't sing anymore," he said. He said it harshly. Not because he meant to, but because he had been thinking of it for so long. "Why?" he asked more gently.

Slowly Papa straightened up. There was a long silence, and the dogs looked up, wondering at it.

"I've forgotten the old songs," said Papa quietly. He sat down. "But maybe there's a way to remember them." He looked up at us.

"How?" asked Caleb eagerly.

Papa leaned back in the chair. "I've placed an advertisement in the newspaper. For help."

—from "Sarah, Plain and Tall

WRITING LETTERS

BEGIN A LETTER with a heading.

- ⊙ The heading should tell your address and the date.
- ⊙ Begin street, city, and state names with capital letters.
- ⊙ Use a comma between the names of your city and state.
- ⊙ Also begin the name of the month with a capital letter.
- ⊙ Use a comma after the number of the day.

USE A GREETING after the heading in a letter.

- ⊙ Begin the word **Dear** with a capital letter.
- ⊙ Begin the name of the person to whom you are writing with a capital letter.
- ⊙ Use a comma at the end of the greeting.

End a letter with a closing and your signature.

- ⊙ Begin the first word in the closing with a capital letter.
- ⊙ Use a comma at the end of the closing.

7880 Webster Street
Buffalo, New York 14242
June 17, 1998

Dear Aunt Claire,

Thank you for taking us to Cooperstown! You know that Roberto Clemente has been one of my heroes for a long time. Getting to see that display about him in the Baseball Hall of Fame Museum was the greatest for me!

Love,
Darrell

USING EDITING AND PROOFREADING MARKS

You can use these editor's marks when you revise and proofread your own writing.

≡	Capitalize.	⌐	Cut something.
⊙	Add a period.	⌒	Replace something.
∧	Add something.	∼	Transpose.
∧	Add a comma.	◯	Spell correctly.
⌄⌄	Add quotation marks.	¶	Indent paragraph.
	/	Make a lowercase letter.	

¶ The judge tapped lightly with her gavel. Her look was stern. The nervous murmuring stopped. In the box, the jury members sat up nervously. If there are any more outbursts," the judge announced, "I shall be forsed to close the courtroom."

CHECK IT OUT

Make Your Own MAGAZINE

TAPE RECORDER

WHITE

Now you have ideas for your magazine title...

PUBLISH!

Name it!

Share your ideas for a magazine title with your classmates. Decide on your title.

Picture it!

If you want, find photos or pictures from old magazines or newspapers, or draw your own. Decide which ones best match the theme of your magazine.

Design it!

Decide where to put your artwork. Now, where will you put your title? Make a small sketch in the Thumbnail box.

Do it!

▶ Cut paper to cover the blue grid on this page.
▶ Arrange your picture on the sheet of paper. Add your title in big, bold letters.
▶ Proofread your front cover and attach it to the blue grid.

THUMBNAIL

 Before beginning, see pages 18 – 19.

contents

Before beginning, see page 105.

Now you have a draft of your introduction...

PUBLISH!

Write it!
Write the final copy of your introduction. Be creative. You can include things like your opinions, your favorite quotation, etc.

Picture it!
Include a photo or drawing of yourself.

Do it!
▶ Cut paper to cover the blue grid on this page.
▶ Write your final copy and arrange your picture on the paper.
▶ Proofread your letter and attach it to the blue grid.

EQUIPMENT

paper

pencils, pens, markers

scissors

glue, paste, or stapler

photos and pictures

creativity

 Before beginning, see page 19.

Now you have a draft of your article...

PUBLISH!

Name it!
Think of titles until you have one that best describes the subject of your article.

Design it!
You have four pages for your article. Plan how you want to use them. Organize your photos or pictures so they help your readers understand the information in your article.

Do it!
▶ Cut paper to cover the blue grid on this page and the next three pages.
▶ Write your final copy and arrange your pictures on the four sheets of paper. Add your title.
▶ Proofread your article and attach it to the blue grids.

EQUIPMENT

paper

pencils, pens, markers

scissors

glue, paste, or stapler

photos and pictures

creativity

Before beginning, see pages 20-21.

in-depth news article

continues!

5

6

in-depth news article

continues!

HBJ material copyrighted under notice appearing earlier in this work.

Proof Your Pages!

▶ Have you placed your copy and illustrations carefully?

▶ Have you read your copy one last time?

▶ Is everything securely attached?

7

opinion article

8

Now you have an opinion...

PUBLISH!

Name it!
Think of a good title for your opinion article.

Share it!
Have a friend take the role of someone who disagrees with your opinion. Use his or her arguments to sharpen your article.

Do it!
▶ Cut paper to cover the blue grid on this page.
▶ Write your final copy on the paper. Add your title.
▶ Proofread your opinion article and attach it to the blue grid.

EQUIPMENT

paper

 pencils, pens, markers

scissors

  creativity

glue, paste, or stapler

Before beginning, see page 38.

Now you have an opinion poll ...

PUBLISH!

Name it!
Choose a title for your opinion poll article.

Picture it!
Now that you've chosen the type of graph you'll use, decide if you want to use colors or patterns to highlight the information.

Write it!
Write out the questions you asked in your poll. Write a summary of your results.

Do it!
▸ Cut paper to cover the blue grid on this page.
▸ Write your final copy and arrange your graphs on the paper. Add your title.
▸ Proofread your opinion poll article and attach it to the blue grid.

EQUIPMENT

paper

pencils, pens, markers

scissors

ruler

glue, paste, or stapler

creativity

 Before beginning, see page 39.

9

Now you have a draft of your story...

PUBLISH!

Name it!
Think of a good title for your story.

Picture it!
Draw pictures to illustrate the important or exciting parts of your story.

Design it!
You have four pages for your story. Plan how you want to use them. Decide how to arrange your pictures and writing. You could set up your pages in two columns, or make borders around the pages.

Do it!
▸ Cut papers to cover the blue grid on this page and the next three pages.
▸ Write your final copy and arrange your pictures on the four sheets of paper. Add your title.
▸ Proofread your story and attach it to the blue grids on pages 10–13.

EQUIPMENT

paper

pencils, pens, markers

scissors

glue, paste, or stapler

creativity

Before beginning, see pages 56-57.

story

continues!

11

story

continues!

12

Proof Your Pages!

▶ Have you placed your copy and illustrations carefully?

▶ Have you read your copy one last time?

▶ Is everything securely attached?

13

how-to article

Now you have a draft of your how-to article...

PUBLISH!

Name it!
Think of a good title for your article.

Picture it!
Illustrate the supplies your readers will need to complete the project.

Design it!
Arrange your instructions and illustrations so the steps in your how-to article are easy to follow.

Do it!
▸ Cut paper to cover the blue grid on this page and the next.
▸ Arrange final copy and illustrations on the paper. Add your title.
▸ Proofread your how-to article and attach it to the blue grids.

EQUIPMENT

paper

pencils, pens, markers

scissors

creativity

glue, paste, or stapler

14

Before beginning, see page 72.

how-to article

continues!

advice column

16

Now you have a draft of your letters...

PUBLISH!

Name it!

Think of a title for your advice column. It can be silly or serious.

Do it!

▶ Cut paper to cover the blue grid on this page and the next.

▶ Write your advice column on the paper. Add your title.

▶ Proofread your advice column and attach it to the blue grids.

EQUIPMENT

paper

pencils, pens, markers

scissors

glue, paste, or stapler

creativity

Before beginning, see page 73.

advice column

continues!

17

poet's corner

18

Now you have your poetry...

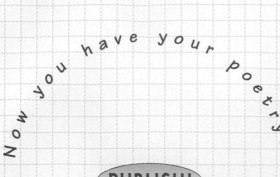

PUBLISH!

Name it!
Think of a title for your "Poet's Corner." Try to match the theme of your poems.

Design it!
Decide where to put your photos or illustrations. Arrange them with the poems. Sketch your design in the Thumbnail box.

THUMBNAIL

Do it!
▶ Cut paper to cover the blue grid on this page.
▶ Arrange your finished poems on the papers.
▶ Creatively arrange the pictures around the poems.
▶ Proofread your poetry and attach it to the blue grid.

EQUIPMENT

paper

pencils, pens, markers

scissors

old magazines or newspapers

glue, paste, or stapler

watercolors or chalk

creativity

Before beginning, see page 88.

Now you have a draft of your interview...

PUBLISH!

Name it!

Think of a good title for your interview.

Picture it!

Draw a picture of your imaginary poet. You could make it a self-portrait!

Do it!

▶ Cut paper to cover the blue grid on this page.
▶ Write your final copy and arrange your pictures on the paper. Add your title.
▶ Proofread your interview and attach it to the blue grid.

EQUIPMENT

paper

pencils, pens, markers

scissors

glue, paste, or stapler

creativity

 Before beginning, see page 89.

Now you have ideas for your career page...

PUBLISH!

Write it!

Use the answers you came up with to write about the career of the month. You can include a description of a typical day on the job.

Do it!

▸ Cut paper to cover the blue grid on this page.
▸ Write your final copy on the paper. Add your illustrations.
▸ Proofread your career page and attach it to the blue grid.

EQUIPMENT

paper

pencils, pens, markers

scissors

glue, paste, or stapler
creativity

Before beginning, see page 104.

Now you have a draft of help-wanted ads...

PUBLISH!

Design it!
Make a sketch of your help-wanted section. Find an eye-catching arrangement for your ads.

Do it!
▸ Cut paper to cover the blue grid on this page.
▸ Write your final copy on the paper.
▸ Proofread your help-wanted section and attach it to the blue grid.

EQUIPMENT
paper

pencils, pens, markers

scissors

ruler

glue, paste, or stapler

creativity

Before beginning, see page 104.

21

Now you have your puzzle...

PUBLISH!

Write it!
Remember to include instructions for your game or puzzle.

Design it!
Make a sketch of your game or puzzle in the Thumbnail box.

Do it!
- ▶ Cut paper to cover the blue grid on this page.
- ▶ Copy your puzzle onto the paper.
- ▶ Proofread your puzzle and attach it to the blue grid.

THUMBNAIL

EQUIPMENT

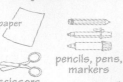

paper

pencils, pens, markers

scissors

ruler

glue, paste, or stapler   creativity

Before beginning, see page 105.

Now you have some weird words...

PUBLISH!

Design it!
Decide how to set up your vocabulary game. Suggestion: list the words in one column and the definitions in another and have your readers draw lines to match words to their definitions.

Write it!
Remember to include instructions.

Do it!
▸ Cut paper to cover the blue grid on this page.
▸ Write your final copy on the paper.
▸ Proofread your vocabulary page and attach it to the blue grid.

EQUIPMENT

paper

pencils, pens, markers

scissors

creativity

glue, paste, or stapler

 Before beginning, see page 105.

23

Now you have ideas for your back cover...

PUBLISH!

Design it!
Decide how to arrange your pictures and illustrations.

Do it!
▶ Cut paper to cover the blue grid on this page.
▶ Arrange your pictures on the paper.
▶ Attach your back cover to the blue grid.

Before beginning, see page 105.